# THE SAGA
# BLUENOSE

*Ernest Fraser Robinson*

**Vanwell Publishing Lir**

**St. Catharines, Ontario**

# DEDICATION

*Jeanne Frances Roué Robinson*

I must go down to the seas again, to the lonely sea and
the sky,
And all I ask is a tall ship and a star to steer her by,
And the wheel's kick and the wind's song and the white
sail's shaking,
And a grey mist on the sea's face and a grey dawn
breaking.

*John Masefield*

Design: Linda L. Moroz, Angela A. Irvine
Map: Loris Gasparotto
Cover Photograph: National Art Limited

Vanwell Publishing Limited
1 Northrup Crescent
P.O. Box 2131
St. Catharines, Ontario   L2R 7S2

Printed in Canada

ISBN 1-55125-009-8 pb
ISBN 0-920277-17-9 hc

# CONTENTS

# INTRODUCTION

## QUEEN OF THE NORTH ATLANTIC

"Ready about!"

The captain's brisk shout alerted his crew that the ship was about to turn through the path of the wind, or "the wind's eye" as sailors call it.

"Hard-a-lee!" he commanded, and the helmsman pushed the ship's wheel firmly to leeward. Canvas sails shook noisily in the 20-knot breeze, and the booms creaked with the strain as the great schooner came about, her lee rail awash and a mist of salt spray spitting out from her bow.

The captain's name was Angus Walters, and the ship was *Bluenose*. The year was 1921, and the schooner with her 20-man crew was headed out from Lunenburg on her first voyage to the great fishing grounds on the Grand Banks.

This voyage was the beginning of a great saga which would span nearly 20 years, and make the schooner *Bluenose* an unforgettable part of our Canadian heritage.

From the sandy shoals of Cape Cod, Massachusetts, to the rocky cliffs of Cape Race, Newfoundland, sailors everywhere came to call *Bluenose* the "Queen of the North Atlantic", the fastest deep-water sailing vessel of her class ever to fish on the great shallow banks that stretch from Boston Bay to the Gulf of St. Lawrence.

She was a large salt water schooner, known in those days as a "salt banker" or "Grand Banker". Her speed made her legendary among the fleets of fishing vessels that worked the Grand Banks in the 1920s and 1930s. She had a graceful long black hull, a curved bow and pointed bowsprit. Her twin masts carried over 930 square metres (10,000 square feet) of canvas. Racing down the wind, salt spray flying as her lee rail cut across the waves, she was a sight never to be forgotten.

For 18 years, from 1921 to 1938, *Bluenose* remained the champion of the North Atlantic fisheries. Challengers from Canada and the United States tried and failed to take the title from her. There were schooners built specifically to beat her, but she refused to give in.

The fame of *Bluenose* spread far and wide. In 1933 she sailed up the St. Lawrence through the Great Lakes to Chicago where she represented Canada all the World's Fair. In 1935 she crossed the Atlantic to England where she was received as a special guest at the Silver Jubilee of George V and Queen Mary.

This proud, graceful sailing vessel became so well known and universally admired for her sleek lines, spectacular rigging and racing qualities that the Canadian government put out a special blue stamp in her honour. Known as the "Fifty-cent *Bluenose* Commemorative", it was issued on January 6, 1929, and is prized by stamp collectors the world over.

*Bluenose* was given additional recognition when her likeness was etched on the back of our Canadian ten-cent piece. The first of these dimes was minted in January, 1937, and the ten-cent piece continues to this day to carry her image, under full sail in a good breeze.

More recently, in November 1988 Canada Post issued a 37-cent commemorative stamp honouring Captain Angus Walters, renowned skipper of *Bluenose*.

This book is the story of *Bluenose*, of how she came to be, of the people who designed and built her, and the men of the sea who sailed her. It is a story every Canadian should know, for *Bluenose* is a part of our rich heritage. Her story can be read with pride, but not without a touch of longing for those spirited times long past.

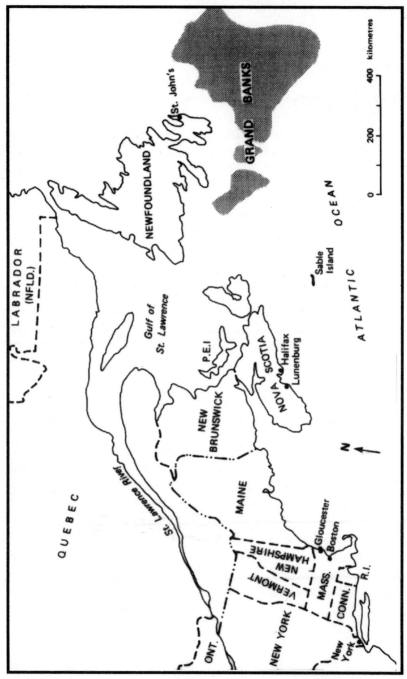

The Fishing Banks.

# CHAPTER 1

## SCHOONERS

The word "schooner" is said to have originated in the New England colonies around 1700, coming from the Scottish word "scoon" or "scon" meaning to skim along the water.

Credit for first using the word in connection with sailing is given to a Scot named Andrew Robinson, a boat builder in Gloucester, Massachusetts. At the launching of one of his ships in 1713, so the story goes, a spectator exclaimed "look how she scons." Robinson, on hearing the comment remarked, "Then a schooner let her be."

At any rate, as applied to sailing vessels built around 1900 to fish in the waters off the coasts of New England, Nova Scotia and Newfoundland, the name "schooner" referred to ships with two masts rigged fore and aft; that is, their main sails lay along the length of the ship from front to rear. Schooners also carried one or more topsails, as well as forward or head sails called jibs.

A typical Grand Banks schooner could carry up to eight sails, amounting in total to as much as 930 square metres (10,000 square feet). The sail plan diagram on page 10 shows all of the sails carried by a Grand Banks fishing schooner such as the *Bluenose*. Schooners seldom put out all their sails when they were fishing on the Grand Banks. The fisherman's stay-

Standing the starboard watch in rough weather.

**Fishing schooners at anchor in Lunenburg harbour.**

sail, a jumbo and a jib, were usually sufficient while working.

The early Nova Scotia schooners, forerunners of the *Bluenose*, were deep, narrow ships which required a lot of extra weight or ballast such as stone, to make them sail effectively. The ballast, of course, took up room and cut down on the carrying capacity of the ship. These schooners, therefore, were not very suitable for carrying freight in the off-season winter months, and proved difficult to sell for the coastal trade when their life as a fisherman was over.

So gradually the Nova Scotia shipbuilders made improvements to the design of their vessels, and by 1910 schooners of more moderate depth, greater stability and more carrying space were being built. Not only could these ships carry more cargo, they proved to be faster sailing with the wind astern, or "off the wind". They also proved to be fairly good sailing into the wind, and were good all round vessels for fishing.

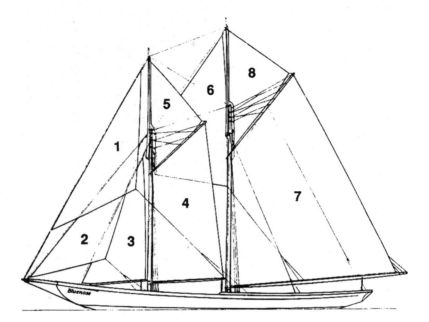

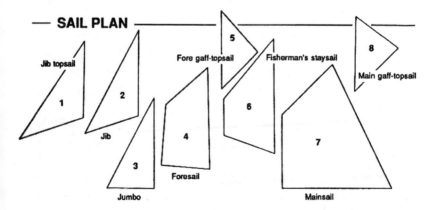

## SAIL PLAN

1 — Jib topsail

2 — Jib

3 — Jumbo

4 — Foresail

5 — Fore gaff-topsail

6 — Fisherman's staysail

7 — Mainsail

8 — Main gaff-topsail

**With her lee rail skimming the surface, a Lunenburg schooner heads for the Grand Banks.**

The fishing schooners built in Massachusetts tended to be different from those built in Nova Scotia, even though they fished the same waters. Some of them were designed to fish all year, and to carry fish back to port as quickly as possible. Narrow vessels with a lot of ballast, they were lower in the freeboard, that is in the distance from the rail of the ship to the waterline, and as a result they tended to get very wet on deck in rough water. Yet they proved to be faster sailing ships into the wind, or "windward"'" as it was called, than the Nova Scotia schooners.

During the fishing season, which lasted from April to September, the schooners would go to the Grand Banks, staying up to eight weeks at a time, or until their holds were full of cod, cleaned and salted down. Some schooners, particularly those from Gloucester, Massachusetts, also fished for fresh fish. They took their catch, packed in ice, and ran

11

for port after only a few days. They had to be fast to keep the fish fresh for market.

The term "Grand Banker" was commonly used along the east coast to describe all the two-masted schooners that were used in the salt cod fishing industry.

These schooners were built of wood, and ranged from 33 to 44 metres (110 to 145 feet) long overall, with a maximum width or beam of 8 to 9 metres (25 to 30 feet), and a depth of 3 to 4.5 metres (10 to 15 feet). The maximum amount of sail carried varied from 740 to 930 square metres (8,000 to 10,000 square feet). Main masts with top masts attached rose over 30.5 metres (100 feet) above the deck.

Speed, of course, depended on the wind and the amount of sail up. Under ideal weather conditions a schooner could exceed 15 knots, which is about 30 kilometres (18 miles) an hour. The number of crew varied, but on the banks it averaged 15 to 20 men, two-thirds of whom were dorymen, those who did the actual fishing. At work a fishing schooner carried 6 to 10 dories, and seldom worked under full sail.

The schooners were sturdy, durable vessels designed and built by men who knew the sea. These ships had to handle all kinds of weather, for the stormy North Atlantic showed no mercy to man or ship. Yet as sound as the schooners were, and as skilled and hardy as were the men that sailed them, many a fishing ship disappeared forever with all hands lost, swallowed up in the fury of a vicious nor'easter.

# CHAPTER 2

## FISHING ON THE GRAND BANKS

"Top dories in the air!"

That sharp command from the schooner's captain would send the dorymen scrambling over the side, be the weather fair or foul. A day's fishing for cod had begun. It may seem to have been a romantic and exciting way of life, but in fact, working on a salt bank schooner on the fishing grounds was a very hard way to earn a living.

You might sign on as one of the dorymen to bait and haul fishing lines, or as a dresser to clean and split the fish, or as a cook. In any of these roles you could expect to put in a 16-hour day, and perhaps longer if you had to stand lookout, or "watch" as it is known.

A working day was from dawn to dark every day, in all kinds of weather. In rough weather, sleep might not come easy in the crowded forecastle which housed the crew of up to 20 men.

The fishing method used by the Lunenburg schooners was known as the dory trawl method. The trawls were lines of strong twine up to 2.5 kilometres (1.5 miles) long. Spaced every 3 metres (10 feet) along the trawl line were three foot lines with hooks on the end. Six to eight of these long trawls would be set out from the schooner by the dorymen, in fan

On a calm morning in the sheltered harbour, the dorymen pull their
schooner out to catch a fresh sea breeze.

shape, with buoys or kegs at the end of each trawl to support it
and to act as a marker. If the weather was good, a schooner
would drop anchor and begin to set trawls before first light.

A typical day aboard a schooner would begin before breakfast with the setting out of the baited trawls by the dorymen
working two to a boat. Tending the trawls was called "under-
running" because, as the line was put out or pulled in, it was
raised up over the dory. The doryman in the bow would raise
the trawl from the water and pass it back to the "afterman",
who would take the fish from the hook, re-bait it, and drop the
line back into the ocean.

It was slow and difficult work, frequently taking up to three
hours just to complete one under-run. It was also very risky
work in bad weather. Dorymen were occasionally lost in fog,
snowstorms or heavy seas.

When a dory completed its run, it returned to the schooner

14

**Back from the Grand Banks.**

with its catch of fish which was hauled on deck and pitch-forked to the gutting tables. Here the dressers cut off the heads of the fish, split them and washed them. They were then placed in the hold and salted down.

Depending on the weather, the trawls would be tended in this manner up to four times a day, before and after breakfast, after dinner and in the early evening, either before or after supper. If the weather caused heavy seas, making it impossible to set out the trawls, the crew would sometimes fish with hand lines, but this method was not very productive.

At the end of each day's work, before the men could climb into their bunks for much needed rest, all the fish had to be properly stored in the holds, and the decks and cutting tables washed down and put "shipshape" as sailors say.

Keeping watch throughout the night was another requirement. The dorymen and dressers had to do this, and they usually worked in shifts of two men. It was extremely important work because there was always the danger of being run down by a passing steamship on its way to New York or London, or colliding with another schooner that had drifted from its moorings.

Captains of fishing schooners had to have a wide range of skills to succeed as fishermen on the Banks. They had to be good navigators to avoid the dangerous reefs and shoals that abound in the area, they had to understand the currents and know where the fish were likely to be at any given time. They had to understand wind and sail, and know how to handle their schooners safely in heavy seas. Most of what they knew had not come from books, but from years of experience on the fishing banks.

Captain and crew worked hard to get a good catch, and to get their fish to port and to market in good time. The amount each crew member earned depended on the amount of fish caught and the price. Some of the crew owned a share of the vessel, a "sixty-fourth" as it was known, which was an added incentive to have the ship earn a profit. Schooners which had the best record for catching fish were called "Highliners".

While the work aboard a fishing schooner was hard and dangerous, and while the profits often depended as much on good luck as on the skills of the captain and crew, it seemed to be a satisfying existence for these rugged and independent men who lived their lives by the sea and knew no other way.

And after all, what could be more thrilling than to be on the deck of a fast salt bank schooner racing down the wind to homeport, all sails up and close-hauled for speed? It was even more exciting when by chance two schooners fell in with one another at sea, and a friendly race began.

# CHAPTER 3

## THE COMPETITION BEGINS

"Up anchor! Up jib and foresail!"

These crisp commands from the schooner's captain signalled that it was time to leave the fishing grounds and head for home, holds filled with gutted cod, split and salted down.

Speed was important now, for getting to port ahead of other schooners meant getting a good berth at the dock, and fetching the best price for the fish.

Hurrying home from the Grand Banks also meant that many a good race developed when schooners met one another at sea. Sometimes they raced simply to relieve the monotony, or provide a break from long hours in the dories or at the gutting tables. These informal races were friendly enough, and made for good discussion in the forecastle at meals or between watches.

Besides their love for the occasional races which took place between them during the fishing season, schooner fishermen from Gloucester to Newfoundland were greatly interested in a regular series of international races for a trophy known as the America's Cup. The United States had held the trophy since 1851, when American yachtsmen won a challenge from the British in a race around the Isle of Wight. At first known as the

100 Guinea Cup, the trophy took the name of *America*, the first winning schooner. The United States retained it against many challengers until 1983, and won it back from Australia in 1987.

In 1919, races for the America's Cup were taking place off Sandy Hook, New York. The British challenger, *Shamrock IV*, had come to regain the trophy from the American defender, *Resolute*, and fishermen all along the east coast followed every detail of the races. In those days, of course, there was no television, and no radio on board most fishing boats, so information on the progress of the races came to schooners on the Banks by word of mouth, from fishermen whose vessels had just arrived.

The Grand Banks fishermen tended to be rather scornful of the vessels that raced for the America's Cup, for they considered them not true deepwater ships but fancy yachts which, in spite of their speed, were not of the quality of the salt water schooners from Gloucester and Lunenburg.

The Lunenburgers called yachts like *Resolute* "tender weather" ships, meaning that they couldn't handle strong winds and rough seas. Lunenburgers and Gloucestermen often talked about the excitement there would be if international races could take place between true sailing ships like the salt bankers.

When it was learned that the American yacht *Resolute* had been declared winner over *Shamrock IV* after the final race was cancelled because of a 23-knot wind, schoonermen everywhere scoffed at the tenderness of those rich men's toys. Fishing schooners worked regularly in breezes like that.

What was needed was a contest between ships that were true sail carriers, ships that could handle heavy weather and not have to run for cover in rising seas. In Nova Scotia, interest became intense in a series of races between what they called "real" sailing ships.

**Schooners racing.**

The answer to their hopes came from Halifax's largest newspaper, the *Halifax Herald*, which offered the International Fishermen's Trophy to be awarded to the fastest fishing vessel on the North Atlantic. An elimination race was to be held off Halifax in the fall of 1920 to determine the champion of the Nova Scotia fishing fleet. Lunenburg alone had over 100 sailing vessels, so competition was bound to be stiff. In Gloucester, Massachusetts, which also had a large fishing fleet, preparations were made for an elimination race to pick an American schooner which could challenge for the trophy.

Unlike the America's Cup, competition for the International Fishermen's Trophy was open only to fishing vessels which had spent at least one season engaged in commercial deep sea fishing prior to the race. And these ships had to have been on the fishing grounds in all kinds of weather from April to September, except for normal trips to port to unload fish or make necessary repairs.

The race itself was to cover a distance of 35 to 40 nautical miles, with a 9-hour time limit to complete the race. The winner would be the schooner that took the best two out of three races, and the prize money would be $5,000.

The Grand Banks fishermen were delighted. Finally there would be a race involving true sailing vessels. Use of sail, ballast, and the skill of captain and crew under a variety of weather conditions would establish the real champion of the North Atlantic.

There was great excitement in Halifax as the date for the elimination races drew closer. Finally, on October 11, 1920, eight vessels from Lunenburg and LaHave started out on a triangular course some 30 miles long. A brisk 20 knot breeze was blowing, and the course was so laid out that all the ships would be tested on their ability to sail against the wind as well as with it.

The schooners seemed to be well matched. All were about 43 metres (140 feet) in length, and carried not less than 840 square metres (9000 square feet) of cotton canvas sail. One of the favorites that day was the *Gilbert Walters*, skippered by Captain Angus Walters of Lunenburg who had earned a reputation as a skillful master on all points of sailing, "on and off the wind" as sailors say. Another able skipper was Captain Thomas Himmelman, whose schooner *Delawanna* was considered one of the finest out of Lunenburg.

It was not to be Captain Walters' day. Although he kept the *Gilbert Walters* on even terms with *Delawanna* up to the last leg of the race, the top foremast on his schooner broke and the vessel fell behind. At the finish *Delawanna* was over five min-

**The Gloucester schooner *Esperanto*, first winner of the International Fishermen's Trophy.**

utes ahead and had established her right to face the American challenger *Esperanto* of Gloucester. They met off Halifax on October 29.

*Esperanto*'s captain was Marty Welch, one of Gloucester's finest sailing masters. Originally a Nova Scotian, he had a reputation for knowing how to get the most out of his sails. At any rate, the race was really no contest. *Esperanto* was an easy winner, taking the first race from *Delawanna* by 18 minutes and the second by 7 minutes.

*Esperanto* took the $4000 first prize money and headed back to Gloucester, much to the dismay of Nova Scotians. Now the United States held both the America's Cup and the International Fishermen's Trophy. It was a sad day for

Maritimers, but there was a determination to win the trophy back as quickly as possible.

Those who knew something about ships and the sea were certain they understood why *Delawanna* lost to *Esperanto*. The New England schooners were built to engage in both the salt cod and fresh fish trade, and therefore were somewhat narrower and lighter than the Lunenburg ships, which stayed on the Banks for longer periods and were heavier and more awkward to handle. The result was that the American schooners sailed better into the wind, and could beat the best the Nova Scotians could produce.

While the Lunenburg schooners were good all-round fishing vessels, it was clear that to beat the American schooners, something new and different had to be designed, something that would be fast both into and against the wind, yet still be able to succeed in the salt fish trade.

That something new would turn out to be the schooner *Bluenose*. She would be designed by a remarkable, self-taught Nova Scotia marine architect named William J. Roué, who became the greatest designer of wooden vessels that Canada ever produced, and one of the greatest sailing ship designers in the world.

# CHAPTER 4

## BLUENOSE IS BORN

At a very early age, young Bill Roué was whittling models of sailboats and trying new ways of putting in ballast to improve their sailing qualities.

"I was making boats when I was four years old, out of shingles - the thin ends. I couldn't cut the thick ends with the table knife," he recalled many years later.

"I had a natural bent for it," he said. "Just as some people have a natural bent for music."

By the age of 12 or 13, he was making models four and five feet long which he sailed for fun on local ponds. It is said that his boats outsailed all the other model ships that came to race.

He was not a particularly good student at school, probably because he was too busy drawing yachts and thinking of keels and waterlines and ballast. His only formal training in the technical skills of ship design was a mechanical drawing course. Everything else about keel and hull he learned by obtaining the best available books on naval architecture and learning them from cover to cover.

At the time of his death at the age of 90, over 250 vessels had been built from Roué designs. In addition he invented and designed sectional barges which were used by the Allied forces in World War 11. Great Britain bought $29 million worth of these barges, and General Dwight Eisenhower, the Commander-in-Chief of the forces in Europe, (who later became President of the United States), said they were superior to all other types of barges being used in the war.

**W.J. Roué,** *Bluenose's* **designer.**

It is interesting to note that while W.J. Roué was an excellent sailor and yachtsman, he never owned a sailing boat of his own. Nevertheless, he earned a reputation as one of the best helmsmen in Canada, and was in great demand to skipper boats owned by others.

The first full-sized sailing boat designed by W.J. Roué was the *Babette,* a small singlemasted vessel launched in 1909. After more than half a century sailing on several east coast harbours, *Babette* is now kept on permanent display at the Maritime Museum of the Atlantic in Halifax, Nova Scotia.

There is a story that when the design of the *Babette* was shown to the famous American boat designer Ben Crowninshield, he studied the plans a while, and then asked who had drawn them. An amateur designer in Halifax, he was told. "Well, he won't be an amateur long," he replied.

In 1909, when W. J. Roué was just beginning his career as a boat designer, there were no naval or marine architects in Nova Scotia, and few if any in all of Canada. Except for designs from England or the United States, ships were almost always built from wooden models.

In those days every local shipyard had its "master builder", a skilled craftsman who, after discussing every detail of a new ship with its future captain or owner, would build a halfmodel (one complete side) to exact scale.

Small pieces of pine would be cut to the correct thickness and carved to the shape required for the boat. Then, when the model was completely satisfactory, experienced shipwrights would build the full sized ship.

This method, however, tended to rely on tried and tested procedures. Major changes in basic design were few. The master builders produced fine schooners like *Delawanna* and *Gilbert Walters*, but what was needed now was a brand new design, one which would combine the fishing qualities of a *Delawanna* with the speed of a Gloucester fisherman like the *Esperanto*. It would take real imagination and skill to design a ship which could win back the International Fishermen's Trophy.

In Halifax, interested businessmen and sportsmen put together a committee to get a design for just such a schooner. W. J. Roué was invited to submit a proposal.

All through the fall of 1920, W. J. Roué worked on his design. He wanted to perfect the underwater lines and the shape of the bow, knowing that the closer he could come to getting those lines right, the closer the ship would come to gliding effortlessly through the water.

With barely three weeks to go before the deadline, he presented his drawings to the Halifax committee. To his dismay they turned down his design, pointing out that his ship had a waterline of 36.6 metres, 2.4 metres too long (120 feet, 8 feet too long) to qualify under the rules for the trophy. He returned to his drawing board and, working day and night, finally came up with a new design that met all the conditions.

To improve the speed of his vessel, W. J. Roué designed it so that the inside ballast on top of the keel would be as low as possible.

"In all other ways," he stated "she is a combination of the Gloucester and Nova Scotia vessels, having the depth of the

25

former and the breadth, freeboard and carrying capacity of the latter."

This time the committee accepted the design. It was decided that the new schooner would be called *Bluenose*, a very common nickname for Nova Scotians, but one of uncertain origins. It may have come from a popular Nova Scotian potato that is nose-shaped and decidedly blue in colour. A more interesting possibility is that described by Dorothy Duncan in her book, *A Portrait of Nova Scotia*. It seems that the name may have come from the activities of a particular Nova Scotia privateer which, during the war of 1812, roamed the waters off the east coast of the United States seizing American ships for their cargo. On the bow of this warship was a cannon painted a bright blue, a feature which not only spread her fame, but led the Americans to insultingly refer to all Nova Scotians as "Bluenosers".

In any case, *Bluenose* would be the name for the new schooner, and she would be built at the shipyards of Smith and Rhuland in Lunenburg where more than 100 of the finest schooners in the North Atlantic fishing trade had been built.

Her keel was laid in the fall of 1920 in a formal ceremony during which the Governor-General of Canada, the Duke of Devonshire, drove a golden spike into the timber. It is said the Governor-General never did actually drive the spike. It seems that while he was being entertained before the ceremony, he had a few drinks too many, so that in spite of several swings of the big iron hammer, he simply could not hit the spike. Eventually it was done for him, and with the keel in place, the hard work of building the ship got started.

A beautifully crafted ship, *Bluenose* was built of Nova Scotia spruce, birch, pine and oak, with masts that were turned from tall Oregon pine. The shipwrights who worked on her were craftsmen who had learned their trade over many years,

FRAME FASTENINGS:

iron drift    iron bolt    wood trunnel
              (riveted)

**Types of frame fastenings, futtocks and board templates, used by early builders.**

their skills passed down to them by their fathers and grandfathers who had been shipwrights before them.

The skills of the shipwrights have become almost a lost art today, and the tools they used such as the adze, the drawknife and the spokeshave are not familiar to us anymore.

The adze was a curved chisel-like blade on a handle, which was used to trim down large timbers into required shapes, such as masts. The spokeshave was used for fine trimming and smoothing rounded surfaces. The booms, gaffs and bowsprit were all carved out by hand by shipwrights using these remarkable tools.

When the last touches were being made in drydock to *Bluenose's* hull, Mr. Smith of the Smith and Rhuland shipyards was asked what he thought of her.

"I don't think nothing of her," he replied. "She is different from any vessel we ever built. We built her as close to the Roué lines as we know how. If she's a success he gets the praise. If she's a failure he gets the blame."

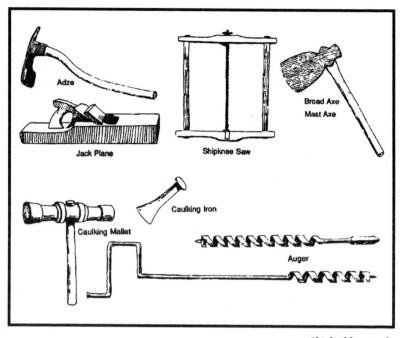

Adze

Jack Plane

Shipknee Saw

Broad Axe
Mast Axe

Caulking Iron

Caulking Mallet

Auger

**Shipbuilding Tools**

Actually there was one alteration made to the original design, the raising of the bow by half a metre (18 inches) in order to allow more room in the forecastle, where the crew would eat and sleep. The captain made the request, and the alteration was made with W. J. Roué's approval.

The result of the alteration was to give the *Bluenose* an unusual sheer or lift in her bow. Some thought it made her look quite ugly, while others thought it gave her a special character which distinguished her from all other fishing schooners of the time.

Some thought the change in the bow was the true reason for her great speed under sail, but W. J. Roué said that all it would

**Keel logs.**

do, if anything, would be to slow her down, except in the roughest of weather when it would help her ride over large waves instead of hammering through them. Some years later, Captain Angus Walters was quoted as saying that had he known the sailing qualities of *Bluenose* he never would have changed her lines.

The matter of the alteration remained controversial for many years, and even today a good argument can be had with oldtimers who saw her in her prime, and like to theorize on what made her so fast a sailing ship.

*Bluenose* was launched at Lunenburg on March 26, 1921. With her two masts in place, or "sticks up", as yachtsmen and sailors describe it, she was handed over to the riggers whose job it was to place the shrouds and halyards, stays, sheets and other running gear. Meanwhile, the sailmaker in his loft com-

*Bluenose* is launched March 26, 1921.

*Bluenose* running down the wind with all sails drawing.

pleted the cutting and sewing of the cotton canvas which would be stretched on the masts.

By early April *Bluenose* was finished. Her dimensions were:

| | |
|---|---|
| Overall length | 43.6 metres (143 ft) |
| Beam | 8.2 metres (27 ft) |
| Waterline | 34.1 metres (112 ft) |
| Draught | 4.85 metres (15 ft,10 in) |
| Mainmast and topmast, above deck | 38.4 metres (125 ft,10 in) |
| Foremast and topmast, above deck | 31.3 metres (102 ft,6 in) |
| Sail area | 930 square metres (10,000 sq. ft) |
| Mainboom | 24.7 metres (81 ft) |
| Foreboom | 9.9 metres (32 ft, 6 in) |
| Displacement | 258.5 tonnes (285 tons) |

It cost $35,000 to build the *Bluenose* in 1921, a figure which is interesting to compare to the nearly $20 million it cost sixty-five years later for Canadians to build an America's Cup yacht only half the size of *Bluenose*.

W. J. Roué's son, James Roué, said that his father's fee for designing the *Bluenose* was $800, but that he did not receive a penny of it! Still, it was an important turning point, for with the building of *Bluenose*, W. J. Roué decided to make the designing of sailing ships his full time career.

# CHAPTER 5

## THE ELIMINATION RACES: OCTOBER 1921

Early in April, 1921, *Bluenose* sailed out of Lunenburg harbour on her sea trials. She proved good on all points of sailing, on and off the wind. On April 15, her racing rigging was replaced with working booms and sails, and she left for the Grand Banks for her first full season of fishing.

The master of the new salt banker was Angus Walters, a crusty, deep-water fisherman from Lunenburg. He was in his thirties in 1921, and had already established himself as a first rate sailor and highline skipper. As captain of the *Gilbert Walters* he had lost out to *Delawanna* in the first elimination series in 1920, but his racing skills in that race had won him much attention.

W. J. Roué recalled Angus Walters as "always a fighter. Nobody put anything over on him in a race." Courageous, daring, and willing to give a schooner all the sail it could carry, the wiry Walters had been sailing since he was 13 years old. From the Grand Banks to the West Indies, he had learned how to get the most out of any ship he skippered. He was an ideal captain for *Bluenose*.

By late September, *Bluenose* had completed her first season on the Banks. It was a successful one. Not only were her supe-

In the 1921 Elimination Series off Halifax, *Bluenose* leads *Canadia*, *Alcala* and *Independence* after the start.

rior sailing qualities proven to her captain and crew, but she had outstanding catches, which qualified her as a highliner in the Lunenburg fleet.

The only question that remained was whether *Bluenose* was good enough to win back the International Fishermen's Trophy from the United States. First she would have to win an elimination race against other Nova Scotia schooners, all eager to be the next challenger.

The elimination races were scheduled to be run off Halifax starting October 15, 1921 . *Bluenose* sailed up from Lunenburg a week early. With a new coat of paint on her hull, and white canvas sails sparkling in the sunlight, she was a thrilling sight to all those who came down to the waterfront to welcome her. Excitement in the city grew as the day of the races approached.

In all there were seven schooners ready to take on *Bluenose* in the best two out of three races. Five of them, including *Delawanna*, were from Lunenburg. Much interest was shown

33

**Racing schooners coming up to a buoy.**

in *Canadia*, a brand new schooner built at Shelburne, Nova Scotia, also just back from her first season on the Banks. Other vessels were the *Alcala* and *Independence* from Lunenburg, and the *Donald J. Cook* from LaHave.

The first race on the 40 mile triangular course was run on Saturday, October 15, in winds that ranged from 8 to 20 knots.

If there had been any doubts about *Bluenose's* racing qualities, they were soon put to rest, as she quickly took the lead and was never headed. Not only was she able to take the lead sailing with the wind to the side and rear, "off the wind" as it is called, but showed that her real talent lay in the hard sailing that takes place when a ship has to sail into the wind. So good was she in this aspect that some called her "a witch to windward".

The final leg of the race was downwind, that is with the wind to the rear. *Bluenose* stayed easily ahead, and passed the finish line over four minutes ahead of *Canadia* her closest competitor. *Delawanna* was even further back, almost 11 minutes off *Bluenose's* winning time of four hours, six minutes and eighteen seconds.

The second race was run on Monday, October 17. The wind was stronger, at 25 knots out of the east-northeast. The result was the same, however, with *Bluenose* beating *Delawanna* by 16 minutes. Again she showed her ability to hold her own off the wind, and run away from the competition sailing into the wind.

Now *Bluenose* had clearly established her right to challenge the American entry for the international trophy. She would not get a chance to race against *Esperanto*, because the speedy Gloucester schooner that had won the cup the previous year by beating *Delawanna* had been lost in a ferocious gale off Sable Island. The Americans had to find another schooner to defend the trophy.

# CHAPTER 6

## THE CHALLENGERS: *ELSIE* 1921

When the American Racing Committee announced that *Mayflower*, a sleek schooner out of Boston, would be the United States' defender in the 1921 series for the International Fishermen's Trophy, fishermen in Lunenburg and Gloucester were angered.

*Mayflower*, in their view, was not a true fishing schooner. She was what was known in those days as a "schooner yacht", a type of vessel designed solely for racing. It was true that *Mayflower* had gone to the Banks to fish in order to satisfy the rules of the competition, but she was not a commercial vessel like *Bluenose* or *Esperanto*, ships whose main business was fishing, not racing.

The Nova Scotians stated flatly that *Mayflower* was not a salt banker, and refused to race against her. The Americans then changed their minds, withdrew *Mayflower*, and quickly planned a series of elimination races to be run off Cape Ann, Massachusetts.

The winner was *Elsie*, a trim and fast fishing schooner out of Gloucester. Although *Elsie* was smaller and lighter than *Bluenose*, she had shown herself to be very fast in all types of sailing conditions. Moreover, her captain was the experienced

Marty Welch, who had won the cup with *Esperanto* the year before, and was one of Gloucester's greatest sailing masters.

The series was to begin on October 22, 1921, on a 64 kilometre (40 mile) course off Halifax. Interest in the contest was intense, and as the day of the first race neared, the main topics of conversation in the city concerned the racing qualities of the two schooners, and how they might perform in different kinds of weather.

*Elsie* sailed up from Gloucester escorted by a United States destroyer. She was a proud, beautiful schooner, with the look of a champion. Hundreds of spectators visited her at dockside for a first-hand look at her size and rigging.

A day or so later, *Bluenose* sailed up the 73 kilometres (45 miles) from Lunenburg. With a fresh coat of paint on her hull, decks scrubbed and white canvas rippling in the harbour breeze, she arrived at her berth with the restless look of a challenger sensing victory, and anxious for the contest to begin.

On her way up the coast, *Bluenose* had met up with *Mayflower*, much to the surprise of both crews. The Boston yacht, having lost her chance to compete for the International Trophy, had decided to come up to Halifax and take in the races anyway.

The two ships then had what sailors call a "brush", a sort of casual race to see which of them might be the faster. *Mayflower* did fall behind in this "brush", but both crews knew it was not a real test for either ship, since *Mayflower* did not have all her racing sails up, and *Bluenose* was not going full out.

Still, it may have partly answered those who said the Nova Scotians were afraid to sail against the speedy *Mayflower*. Experienced sailors were certain *Bluenose* would have won a series with *Mayflower*, believing that the Boston schooner yacht was a tender weather vessel that would not perform as

*Elsie* **losing foretopmast.**

well as *Bluenose* in all kinds of weather.

Anyway, in the crowded quarters of a fishing schooner's forecastle, arguments on such weighty matters as these tended to ease the boredom of the long days and nights at sea.

The first race of the 1921 series got underway in brisk 25 knot winds, out of the northwest. With gusts up to 35 knots, the seas were heavy, and waves reached 6 metres (20 feet) or more.

*Elsie* was first off the starting line and held the lead for about 9.7 kilometres (6 miles) before *Bluenose*, sailing into the wind, pulled ahead. But the race remained close until the last leg when *Bluenose*, pushed by winds up to 27 knots, sped down to the finish line well ahead.

About two-thirds of the way through the race, *Elsie's* fore topmast snapped in a gust of wind. Though the loss of sail may have slowed her slightly, it was too late to affect the outcome

**38**

**The captain of the *Bluenose,* Angus Walters of Lunenburg,
with the International Fishermen's Trophy.**

of the race. In fact, as soon as Captain Angus Walters saw what
had happened to *Elsie*, he reduced *Bluenose's* sail so there
would be no advantage to his own vessel.

*Bluenose* finished the race about 12 minutes ahead of *Elsie*.
To the delight of Nova Scotians, the Lunenburg schooner had
shown a remarkable ability to handle rough weather, particularly sailing into the wind. But would she do it again? Marty
Welch and *Elsie* would not give up easily.

The second race, on Monday, October 24, took place in
much lighter weather. The winds were still out of the northwest, but only at 10 -12 knots.

39

With a new foretopmast in place, *Elsie* again got off to a good start, and was leading *Bluenose* as the schooners neared the last leg and the run for the finish line. Now, however, they were sailing to windward, and again *Bluenose* proved unbeatable. In short turns called tacks, Captain Walters moved his schooner back and forth across the face of the wind, quickly making up all the distance lost to *Elsie*. *Bluenose* crossed the finish line 10 minutes in the lead.

*Bluenose* had done it! The International Fishermen's Trophy was back in Nova Scotian hands, and honour had been restored.

Interest in the schooner races reached new heights with the victory of *Bluenose*. Ship to shore radio was used for the first time to describe a sailing event such as this, and now everyone could follow the progress of the race as it actually happened.

There were parties around the city. At some, champagne flowed freely, and fiddlers spun out snappy reels and jigs. There is a story that a bottle of champagne was sent down to the *Bluenose*, but the Lunenburg sailors didn't think much of it.

The heck with this apple juice," one sailor is said to have remarked. "Let's have a real drink." So out came a keg of rum.

*Elsie* had given a good account of herself in the 1921 series, but it had not been enough against the spirited *Bluenose*. The next series was set to be raced in American waters. Now it was up to the Americans to design and build a fast, new schooner that could bring the trophy back to the United States.

# CHAPTER 7

## THE CHALLENGERS: *HENRY FORD* 1922

In Gloucester that winter, conversation was mainly about schooners and racing. *Elsie's* loss to *Bluenose* had sorely damaged the town's pride. Local shipbuilders were determined to win back the trophy the very next year, and by December work on two brand new schooners was underway.

One of the new vessels was *Puritan*, a handsome schooner designed by W. Starling Burgess, the world famous American marine architect. *Puritan* proved so fast in her sea trials, even in rough weather, that she seemed to be a good bet to beat *Bluenose*. Sadly, she was not to get the chance to prove herself. Her speed made her hard to handle, and in June 1922, on her third trip to the fishing grounds, she ran aground and sank on a reef off Sable Island.

The second schooner to come from the shipyards at Gloucester that winter was *Henry Ford*, a strong looking vessel with beautiful lines. She was designed by Thomas McManus, a captain who had drawn the plans of more than a hundred fishing schooners. *Henry Ford* was 41.8 metres (137 feet) in length, compared to *Bluenose's* 43.6 metres (143 feet), and carried slightly less sail than the Grand Banker from Lunenburg.

*Bluenose* **during races.**

Before her masts could be set in place and her rigging installed, *Henry Ford* had problems that led some people to think she might be jinxed. At her launching, she broke free of her tow lines and ran aground. The damage was minor, but the accident may have reduced her overall sailing ability, particularly with her sails which had to be cut back in size to meet the standards of international racing competition.

However, *Henry Ford* had no trouble at all proving her superior speed and sailing ability in the American elimination races held off Gloucester in October, 1922. She easily won over her three competitors, including the Boston schooner *Yankee*, which like *Henry Ford* had been specially designed to outsail the *Bluenose*.

Captained by Clayton Morrissey, an experienced Gloucester

skipper, *Henry Ford* now made final preparation for the international races scheduled to begin on October 21 on the Cape Ann triangle near Gloucester.

Meanwhile at Halifax, three Nova Scotia schooners – *Mahaska, Canadia*, and *Margaret K. Smith* – arrived to challenge *Bluenose* for the right to defend the International Fishermen's Trophy against the Americans.

*Mahaska* was a new Lunenburg schooner thought by her owners to be faster than *Bluenose*. She also had the advantage of having the letter "a" appear three times in the spelling of her name. According to an old fishermen's superstition, this would bring her good luck. *Canadia's* owners must have believed the same superstition.

The good luck omens failed to be of any help, however, as *Bluenose* won easily in a 48 kilometre (30 mile) race run on October 2. At the finish, *Bluenose* led *Canadia* by 6 minutes and *Mahaska* by 20. There could be no doubt of *Bluenose's* superior racing qualities. She would defend the cup. Paddy Mack, captain of the *Mahaska*, is said to have been so angry at the loss to *Bluenose* that he threw his cap down on the deck and jumped up and down on it. Whether he was mad at himself or *Bluenose* is not known.

By the middle of October, *Bluenose* was ready to sail down to Gloucester for the series with *Henry Ford*. Escorted by the Canadian destroyer H.M.C.S. *Patriot*, she arrived in Gloucester harbour to find the port in a mood of high excitement. Gloucester pride and American honour were at stake in the upcoming races.

Winds were light on the day of the first race, and the official racing committee decided to delay the start until breezes picked up. But *Bluenose* and *Henry Ford* were already at the start line, their sails set and their crews eager to start. The two

**Off Gloucester in the 1922 series, *Henry Ford* leads *Bluenose*
at the start of a race.**

captains, ignoring the signal to wait, nodded to one another that
they were ready to go, and the race was on despite the committee. Schooner captains were free spirited, independent men
used to making up their own minds. They didn't like depending on committees to decide whether it was racing weather.

The light breezes off Gloucester that day did not favour
*Bluenose*, and it was *Henry Ford* that crossed the finish line
first. But the race had taken longer than the approved time
limit, which meant that the result would not have been allowed
to stand, even if the start had been legal.

Angus Walters was satisfied that *Henry Ford* had won in a
fair race, and was willing to see the victory made official.
However, the racing committee remained firm in its view that

44

the rules had to be followed. The race would not count!

The crew of *Henry Ford*, perhaps forgetting that not just the false start, but the extended time, broke the rules of the competition, threatened to quit. Fortunately they changed their minds when an official of the United States government reminded them that quitting would bring dishonour to Gloucester and the United States.

Hot tempers quickly cooled and both crews settled down to the business of deciding a winner. It took three more races to do it.

*Henry Ford* won the first of them by more than 2 minutes, again in light winds. Winds picked up for the next two races, and in brisk breezes of 20-25 knots, *Bluenose* beat *Henry Ford* by over 7 minutes each time.

It was clear, even to the Americans, that *Henry Ford* was a tender weather schooner. She was able to handle *Bluenose* in light winds, but simply could not stay with her when the breezes picked up.

When some disappointed supporters of *Henry Ford* complained that the weather had not been fit to race in, Angus Walters replied that it was, after all, just a "smooth weather blow". True enough, it was typical weather for a Grand Banks schooner, and no member of *Henry Ford's* crew was heard to make any complaint about the winds.

American hopes were dashed. Gloucestermen shook their heads in dismay. Proudly, *Bluenose* sailed home to Lunenburg with the prize money and the International Fishermen's Trophy. No lucky upstart was this Nova Scotia schooner! She was every inch a champion, and it would take a champion to beat her.

# CHAPTER 8
## THE CHALLENGERS:
## *COLUMBIA* 1923

American feelings may have been badly bruised by the 1922 loss to *Bluenose*, but the desire to win back the international trophy burned as fiercely as ever.

Shipbuilders in Gloucester, remembering *Puritan*, the speedy schooner that had been lost at sea before she had a chance to race *Bluenose*, turned to W. Starling Burgess, *Puritan's* designer, to draw the plans for another schooner, one which would have *Puritan's* speed and be able to match *Bluenose* sailing into the wind. They wanted a champion, and would spare neither effort nor expense.

The result was *Columbia*, one of the most beautiful schooners ever built, and perhaps the best of all the American challengers for the International Fishermen's Trophy. She was launched at Gloucester in the spring of 1923.

*Columbia's* trim lines and proud look gave her an elegance similar to that of *Bluenose* herself. Actually, she was 5.5 metres (18 feet) shorter than *Bluenose*, even though she carried almost as much sail. Some, like Angus Walter, thought she carried too much sail for her size, and would be slower as a result.

In her sea trials she was fast, and showed she could sail well in all kinds of weather. She scored an easy win over *Henry*

*Columbia.*

*Ford* in the elimination races off Gloucester in the fall of 1923. Her captain was Ben Pine, a Gloucester skipper as tough minded and determined to win as Angus Walters himself.

The 1923 races for the International Fishermen's Trophy were scheduled to be run off Halifax beginning October 29. *Columbia* came up two days early, and was met by excited crowds who greatly admired her handsome lines. The strengths and weaknesses of *Columbia* and *Bluenose* were argued endlessly, as were the racing style and talents of the two masters, Ben Pine and Angus Walters. Interest had reached fever heat by the time the two schooners met at the starting line.

At 11:30 on the morning of October 29, in winds of 6 to 17

knots out of the west southwest, the starting gun for the first race was fired. *Bluenose* took an early lead, but the schooners were dead even by the time they reached the final stretch down to the finish line.

It was a fight to the finish, with no quarter asked or given by crew or captain on either vessel. Entering this last stretch for home, which sailors call the "reach", the two schooners raced head to head down the wind, all sails up and drawing every inch of breeze they could get.

Each schooner struggled for an advantage. *Columbia* stayed to leeward on the left or port side of *Bluenose*, blocking her from moving out with the wind to take the lead. But so close were the two vessels that this tactic by *Columbia* forced *Bluenose* closer to shore, into shallow waters where there was risk of running aground.

Already *Bluenose* had narrowly missed hitting the famous "Three Sisters" shoal, one of the worst reefs along the coast, and now, at a speed of nearly nine knots, she was fast approaching other rocky shallows. With *Columbia*, holding to her course, *Bluenose* had no choice but to veer away from the reefs, even at the risk of a collision.

"Bear away!" came the command.

The helmsman spun the wheel and *Bluenose* swung out towards *Columbia*. It was a near miss, but the schooners did not collide. However, as *Bluenose* moved across *Columbia's* bow, her main boom swung around and caught in *Columbia's* shrouds. For almost a minute *Bluenose* pulled *Columbia* behind her. Then just as quickly, she broke free and raced easily into the lead, finishing the race one minute and twenty seconds ahead.

Under the rules, *Columbia* could have protested the race on the grounds that *Bluenose* had snared her rigging. But there had been little choice after *Columbia* had pushed her so close to shore. Captain Ben Pine understood this, and did not lodge a protest. The first race went to the Canadian champion.

The racing committee decided to make sure that dangerous situations like this would not occur again. It ruled that all marker buoys along the course of the race were to be passed on the seaward side, which would keep the racing schooners away from the shore. A list of all the buoys concerned was given to each captain.

Light winds delayed the races for several days, but finally, on Thursday, November 1, with brisk 25 knot winds out of the northeast, the second race began. The weather and stiff breezes were ideal for *Bluenose*, and she made the race look easy. Showing her remarkable ability to sail into the wind, she beat *Columbia* by nearly three minutes. Having won two races and the series, *Bluenose* prepared to sail home to Lunenburg.

Then Angus Walters learned that Ben Pine had lodged a protest. *Bluenose* had broken the new rule set out by the committee. She had passed one marker buoy on the landward side.

It was true. But Walters argued that it hadn't made any difference to the outcome: *Bluenose* hadn't interfered with *Columbia* or gained any advantage in distance by passing the marker on the wrong side. Besides, said Walters, the marker was not one that warned of dangerous shoals. The committee did not accept the arguments, however. *Bluenose* had broken the rules. The race was awarded to *Columbia*.

To say that Angus Walters was angry would be putting it mildly. From his point of view, *Bluenose* had won two races, enough for victory in the series, and that was that. However, he did agree to carry on with the series if the race was simply declared a "no race", rather than being awarded to *Columbia* When the committee refused this offer, Walters hoisted sail and

**49**

took *Bluenose* back to Lunenburg. The committee announced that no winner would be declared for the series, and awarded half the prize money to *Columbia*. *Bluenose* kept the trophy.

A lot of bad feeling resulted from the 1923 series. While the Gloucester schooner had not been able to beat *Bluenose*, the Americans believed the Nova Scotians had not beaten *Columbia* either, at least not fair and square. For their part, the Nova Scotians said that *Columbia* had been clearly beaten twice in a row by *Bluenose*, and the Americans simply didn't want to admit that they couldn't build a ship good enough to beat *Bluenose*.

So strong were the feelings on both sides, that eight years passed before another series of races for the International Fishermen's Cup could be arranged.

This break in international racing competition did not mean that interest in schooner racing died out. In fact, there were shipbuilders and sportsmen in Nova Scotia already planning to design and build a schooner to challenge the North Atlantic champion. Meanwhile *Bluenose*, with her title intact and the trophy secure in Lunenburg, returned to her main job of fishing for cod on the Grand Banks.

# CHAPTER 9

## THE CHALLENGERS: *HALIGONIAN* 1926

Even with such cleverly designed and skillfully built schooners as *Henry Ford* and *Columbia*, the Americans had been unable to defeat *Bluenose*. Was it possible that Nova Scotians themselves could build a vessel that would outsail her?

A group of Halifax businessmen decided to take that question to the one man they thought would have the answer, W. J. Roué. When the young designer said he could indeed design such a schooner, the Halifax group at once agreed to put up the money. Shipbuilders in Shelburne were ready to do the construction, and so Roué immediately set to work to produce the drawings, using ideas and improvements that had been in his mind for some time.

Christened *Haligonian*, the new schooner was launched at the Shelburne shipyards in March, 1925. In several ways she was similar to *Bluenose*, having about the same length, the same width at the waterline, and carrying the same amount of sail. Her lines and ballast were different, however. She was built much lower in the bow, a change which tended to make her cut through high waves rather than ride over them. Racing in heavy seas, her decks were usually awash, making her a "wetter" ship than the high-riding *Bluenose*.

**Bluenose leads *Haligonian* at the start of a race in their 1926 series.**

During the spring and summer of 1925, *Haligonian* had a good first season on the Banks. Late in the season, however, she ran into bad luck. Returning to port loaded with saltcod, she had the misfortune to run aground on a gravel reef in the Strait of Canso.

Repairs were made to her during the winter, but experienced seafarers said she was never the same afterwards. As they put it, *Haligonian* was "hogged", meaning that her bow and stern ends had sagged slightly. Today we might say that the accident put her alignment out, for she now had what sailors called a "lee helm", that is a tendency to turn away from the wind. At any rate, the 1925 races with *Bluenose* had to be cancelled while repairs to *Haligonian* were carried out.

*Bluenose* had her own share of bad luck that year. Fishing on the Banks, she damaged her hull when she went aground on a rocky shoal near the coast of Newfoundland. And in April, 1926, on her way out to the fishing grounds, she took a bad beating in a heavy gale off Sable Island.

Captain Angus Walters, referring to the storm, said that *Bluenose* faced "the grandmother of all seas". Sails ripped, deck rails snapped, and heavy cables and rope lines were torn loose. For seven hours *Bluenose* was hammered by heavy winds and high waves. Exhausted and bruised, she was finally able to scamper to safety.

At last, in October 1926, *Haligonian* and *Bluenose* met at Halifax in a best two out of three series of races. The skipper of *Haligonian* was Captain Moyle Crouse of Lunenburg. He and the backers of *Haligonian* had high hopes their new schooner would be more than a match for *Bluenose*.

But *Haligonian* did not handle well. In the first race *Bluenose* beat her by 30 minutes, a crushing defeat for the Shelburne schooner. The next two races went over the time limit and didn't count, although *Bluenose* finished in the lead both times. On Wednesday, October 20, *Bluenose* won the final race, this time by seven minutes. Again the speedy Lunenburger had turned away a challenger specially built to beat her.

There are those who argue, even today, that *Haligonian* did have the qualities to beat *Bluenose*. They claim that *Haligonian*, when loaded with fish, did indeed sail faster than *Bluenose*, and insist that had she carried more ballast when racing or distributed it differently, she would have won.

But the two ships never met again, and so the debate goes on. It is certain, however, that *Haligonian* did not defeat *Bluenose* when she had her chance to do so.

Back in Gloucester, meanwhile, hope had not died that the International Fishermen's Trophy could be brought back to the United States. There was growing interest in building yet another schooner to take on *Bluenose*.

# CHAPTER 10

## THE CHALLENGERS:
## *GERTRUDE L. THEBAUD*
## 1930, 1931

The last American challenge to *Bluenose* came from a lean and spirited schooner built at the Essex shipyards near Gloucester during the winter of 1929-1930. She was named *Gertrude L. Thebaud*, after the wife of a wealthy Frenchman who spent his summers in Gloucester, and who contributed $30,000 to the cost of building her.

Usually known simply as *Thebaud*, with the 'h' and 'd' not sounded, as in the French pronunciation, she was designed by a firm of Boston architects and launched in March 1930. *Thebaud* was a trim, handsome deepwater fishing schooner built to race. Some thought she had a yacht-like appearance, with her tall masts, sharp bow and short bowsprit. Sailors recognized her by the high main gaff, the top spar that carried her large topsail.

*Thebaud* was a smaller schooner than *Bluenose* in overall length, width, and depth, and carried only 720 square metres (7,730 square feet) of sail, compared to *Bluenose's* 930 (10,000). Lunenburg captains like Angus Walters thought even that was too much sail for her size, a common fault, in their opinion, of most of the Gloucester schooners. *Thebaud's* captain was Ben Pine, the determined Gloucester skipper who had been master of *Columbia* in the 1923 series.

As *Thebaud* was being outfitted with her rigging in the spring of 1930, the town of Gloucester was busy planning celebrations to mark its 300th anniversary. As one of the events to honour the occasion, it was decided to hold an international schooner race. A challenge was sent to *Bluenose* to race *Thebaud* in a series to be run off Gloucester in October, after the end of the fishing season. The International Fishermen's Cup would not be at stake, but a new cup, the Lipton Trophy, would be awarded to the winner.

It was a tough decision for Angus Walters and the *Bluenose* crew. After 10 years fishing on the Grand Banks, their schooner was showing signs of wear and tear. Her planks had absorbed a lot of water over that time, and she sat lower in the water than she should.

Her scrapes with rocky reefs and sand bars on trips to and from the fishing grounds had left her scarred, and altered her ballast. Her sailing ability was probably less than it used to be. Nevertheless, *Bluenose* had never refused a challenge. So, outfitted with a new set of sails, off she went to do battle with *Thebaud*.

From the start things did not go well. During the trip down to Gloucester, *Bluenose* ran into heavy winds which stretched her new canvas sails. As a result, in the first race over the 40 mile course, she did not handle well. *Thebaud* finished ahead by about 15 minutes, a major defeat for the Lunenburg schooner.

Repairs were quickly made to her sails, and *Bluenose* looked ready to do much better. Unfortunately, the second race had to be cancelled several times because the winds were either too light or too heavy. On two occasions, *Bluenose* had taken the lead when the race was called off. Such delays were frustrating to the crews of both schooners.

Finally, on October 18, the weather was suitable. *Bluenose* took the early lead, and was ahead by five minutes at the halfway point. Then Captain Walters made a move which likely cost *Bluenose* the race. Rather than holding to his course, he moved closer to shore, hoping to pick up a fresh breeze rising out of the northwest.

It didn't happen, and *Bluenose* soon fell behind. At the finish *Thebaud* led by eight minutes.

Angus Walters admitted his error. "She didn't beat the *Bluenose*," he said later. "She beat me."

But the reason didn't matter. *Bluenose* had lost, and lost decisively. There was joy in Boston and Gloucester. At last the Americans had found a winning schooner. Now to get back the International Fishermen's Trophy!

Quickly Gloucester issued a challenge for the trophy. It was accepted, and a series was scheduled to be raced off Halifax the following year. The Americans could hardly wait for *Thebaud* to bring an end to *Bluenose's* long reign as champion. From Boston to Bar Harbor, Yankee salt fishermen could taste victory.

Nova Scotians accepted the loss as gracefully as they could. They were not certain that *Thebaud* had really proven her sailing superiority, but there were nagging doubts in their minds about *Bluenose*. Was she too old to compete any more? Had she been battered by too many storms on the Grand Banks? They knew that even the best of champions couldn't last forever. They also knew the answers to their questions would be given in a year's time in the waters off Halifax.

In late October, 1931, *Gertrude Thebaud* sailed confidently up to Halifax. She made the trip in record time, and Captain Ben Pine said straight out that he had come to win.

In light winds, *Bluenose* and *Thebaud* ran their first race on

Saturday, October 31. *Bluenose* was 35 minutes ahead when she crossed the finish line, but the time allowance had been exceeded and the race did not count.

On Monday they went at it again, and this time it was official. *Bluenose* won by more than 32 minutes, a clear cut victory. *Thebaud* seemed to be having trouble with her sails, and Ben Pine said her ballast was not right. But *Bluenose*, in spite of her advanced years, had sailed like a spunky two-year-old.

Captain Angus Walters, pleased to have made up for his loss to *Thebaud* a year earlier, could hardly resist poking a little fun at the Gloucester schooner. He remarked that it got very lonely out there without another schooner in sight to keep *Bluenose* company!

The next day, in brisk winds gusting up to 20 knots, *Bluenose* won easily, crossing the finish line with a lead of 12 minutes. The two victories removed all doubts about the racing qualities of the aging schooner. She was still the best. The International Fishermen's Trophy would stay in Nova Scotia. In Lunenburg, proud townsmen held a victory parade to welcome back *Bluenose* and her crew.

Boston and Gloucester were shocked at the loss. They really had expected *Thebaud* to win. To ease the blow they expressed the view that now the series between the two schooners was tied, *Thebaud* having won in 1930, and *Bluenose* in 1931. The big question was whether there would ever be a deciding match.

A final contest between the two great schooners may have been desirable, but it seemed unlikely to happen after the 1931 races. For one thing, in the fishing ports along the eastern coast of Canada and the United States, diesel engines were fast replacing sail as the chief means of power. Also, trawling and dragging were found to be more profitable ways to fish than the time-consuming dory method used by the sailing schooners.

To top it off, the fresh fish market was now more important than the salt cod industry, particularly in the United States. Fishing schooners like *Bluenose* and *Thebaud* were disappearing from the fishing banks. *Thebaud* was the last schooner of her type built in Gloucester, and even she had been designed with a built-in engine. In 1936, *Bluenose* herself was to have diesel engines installed.

As it turned out, *Bluenose* and *Thebaud* did meet again. But seven years would pass before destiny brought them together for the last time, in a duel which settled forever the question of which of them was truly "Queen of the North Atlantic".

# CHAPTER 11

## WORLD RECOGNITION

After the victory over *Thebaud*, *Bluenose* returned to her work as a fishing schooner. It was becoming more difficult every year to make a profit in the salt cod industry, but the owners of *Bluenose* continued to insist that she be able to pay her own way. Her growing fame had not lessened the cost of keep-

**The 50-cent *Bluenose* stamp issued in 1929. It was based on a photograph of *Bluenose* series off Halifax in 1926.**

ing her in good sailing condition. In 1929, the Government of Canada decided to recognize the attention and respect *Bluenose* had gained for Canada by issuing a new stamp in her honour. It was a blue 50-cent stamp, and showed *Bluenose* racing off Halifax harbour in 1926. The stamp was in great demand from the day it was issued, and now can be found only in the hands of collectors.

By 1931, the name *Bluenose* was known around the world.

*Bluenose,* an honoured guest at the 1933 Chicago World's Fair.

From the Caribbean to the South China Sea, there were salt water sailors who had heard about the swift Nova Scotian vessel, and how for a decade she had outsailed every schooner that ventured forth to challenge her in the wind-swept North Atlantic.

In fact, so famous had *Bluenose* now become that in 1933 she was invited to represent Canada at the World's Fair that summer in Chicago.

Up the St. Lawrence *Bluenose* sailed, through Lake Ontario and the Welland Canal to Lake Huron, Lake Michigan, then south to Chicago. Thousands came to visit her and admire her sleek lines and smart rigging. Some were fortunate enough to be on board for short sailing excursions.

Although it had been a long and expensive trip for

*Bluenose*, financially it was a success, for admission fees more than offset the costs of operation. On the return voyage, *Bluenose* stopped at Toronto where she remained through the winter and spring. Again she was visited by thousands of admiring spectators, many of whom came to dockside to be able to say in later years that they had seen the beautiful schooner at the height of her career.

In the summer of 1934 she sailed back to Lunenburg. By that time so many had walked the decks that her planks had to be replaced before she could resume her work on the fishing grounds.

The next year, 1935, *Bluenose* received another invitation that recognized her fame. She was asked to go to England to represent Canada at the Silver Jubilee of King George V and Queen Mary.

It took 17 days for *Bluenose* to make the trip across the Atlantic to the port of Plymouth. On her arrival, crowds of spectators gathered to give her a warm welcome. A proud moment came when she took part in a great sailpast at Spithead, as the King formally reviewed the British home fleet. Afterwards, Captain Walters was invited on board the Royal Yacht to meet the 70-year-old monarch.

"He was a very nice, ordinary sort of fella," recalled the Captain. "We chewed the rag a while."

The racing qualities of *Bluenose* were well-known in England, and so during her visit, the Nova Scotia schooner was invited to take part in an exhibition race with several British yachts. Captain Walters knew the British vessels were schooner-yachts, designed only for racing, and that *Bluenose*, a fishing schooner, could not be expected to do well against them. He agreed to race, however, and brought *Bluenose* across the line in third place, a fine showing for the Nova Scotian

Grand Banker.

On September 11, 1935, *Bluenose* sailed for home. Barely 24 hours out of port she ran headlong into one of the worst gales ever experienced by Captain Walters and his crew. Winds of hurricane force stirred up high waves that pounded at her for three straight days. Her strength was tested to the limit.

"Everything was afloat down below," Angus Walters recalled later, "and when the biggest sea of all hit us to leeward, I thought it was the end. *Bluenose* staggered under the blow and keeled right over – stayed under for some time due to the weight of water she was carrying – and then gradually righted herself."

"I have been at sea for 30 years," he continued, "but I have never seen anything like the seas that night. If they had continued another hour, we should have had to cut away the masts. Both our boats were smashed to pieces."

A British naval commander who was on board for the trip to Nova Scotia and who had 17 years of experience in destroyers and seen many a bad storm made the following comment:

"This was the most terrifying sea I have ever encountered. That we are alive today is a tribute to the seamanship of Captain Angus Walters and his crew, and the wonderful qualities of *Bluenose*."

With sails shredded, masts lost, her booms and rigging torn away, *Bluenose* finally limped into the port of Plymouth a sorry sight, but with no lives lost. She remained a month in the docks at Plymouth before repairs could be finished to make her seaworthy. Then she sailed back to Lunenburg where more work had to be done before she could get back to the fishing grounds.

By 1936, heavily in debt due to falling profits in the salt cod trade, and with her owners starting to talk of selling her off to the coastal trade, *Bluenose* had her topmasts taken down and diesel engines installed. This was not a happy event, but simply had to be done if she was to have any hope of holding her own in the fishing business. At least the engines were installed in such a way that they could be easily removed should there ever be another race.

But *Bluenose* was now 16 years old. Water-logged and bent, she had been pounded in too many storms, and was clearly past her prime. There had been no challengers since *Thebaud* in 1931. Nor were there any new schooners being built to face the aging Queen. In 1936, prospects for another great race seemed dim indeed.

**In November 1988 Canada Post issued a commemorative stamp honouring Capt. Angus Walters.**

# CHAPTER 12

## THE LAST CHALLENGE: *THEBAUD* 1938

*Gertrude Thebaud*, the famous Gloucester schooner, was also present at the World's Fair in 1933. Like *Bluenose*, she came to Chicago by way of the St. Lawrence River and the Great Lakes. And, like *Bluenose*, she proved to be a great attraction at the fair, drawing many thousands of visitors. It is not surprising that the presence of both these great schooners caused renewed interest in seeing them race again.

When *Thebaud* returned to Gloucester in the fall of 1933, talk had already begun about another try at winning back the International Fishermen's Trophy. Interest grew during the next few years, particularly in Boston where experienced schooner sailors believed that the aging *Bluenose* would not be able to withstand another challenge from *Thebaud*, 8 years old and in her prime.

As well, sportsmen in the Boston area were convinced that there would be tremendous national and international interest in such an event, especially if it were sailed in American waters, preferably at Boston which had not hosted any of the international schooner races.

Finally, in 1937, the Americans challenged *Bluenose* to meet *Thebaud* in a best of five series of races for the

International Fishermen's Trophy. The races would be sailed in the fall of 1938 on courses off Boston and Gloucester. First prize would be worth $3,000 and second prize $2,000.

Captain Angus Walters was ready to accept the challenge, but there were serious financial concerns. *Bluenose* had to be completely refitted, since most of her gear had been stored away after the installation of diesel engines in 1936. Topmasts had to be put back in place, and new running gear, including some sails and lines, had to be purchased. The diesel engines had to be removed, and there were many other costs involved in getting the old ship ready for competition again.

Difficulty in raising the money to cover these costs nearly stopped the owners of *Bluenose* from going ahead. In those days, governments did not offer funds to help in sporting events, even though a new ten-cent piece with *Bluenose's* image on one side had been minted by the government in 1937 in honour of the famous schooner. No government funds were offered now to help her race again. It was solely up to private interests. Finally, the Americans agreed to offset some of the expenses if *Bluenose* accepted the challenge. She did, and the race was on.

With planking that groaned from the beating of a thousand heavy seas, and a hull grown soft from the strain of 18 years on the fishing banks, *Bluenose* struggled to get herself together for the contest with *Thebaud*.

When she sailed into Gloucester harbour in October that year, she looked trim and ready to run. The odds were against her, but she was a proud schooner sailed by proud men. *Bluenose* had come as a champion and intended to sail like one.

One of her crew for that 1938 series was a young Lunenburg sailor named Arthur Corkum. Years later he recalled the thrill of his experience.

"I remember how excited I was to be among that group as we sailed for Gloucester," he recalled.

"Captain Angus Walters assigned me to tend the topsails high up in the cross-trees. I will never forget it. We encountered a storm with 25 knot winds and heavy rain, so it was quite the task for my first time tending the topsails. I think Angus assigned me to the topsails because I was young, agile and could climb well." Corkum thought highly of Captain Walters.

"Angus didn't stand for any fooling," he remembered. "But he was fair and reasonable and knew the *Bluenose* like the back of his hand. You almost sensed he could communicate with her."

The first race was sailed off Boston harbour on October 9. *Bluenose* had trouble with her bowsprit and rigging, and did not sail well. *Thebaud* crossed the finish line a winner by nearly three minutes, much to the joy of her Boston backers.

Unsuitable weather delayed the next race for several days, but this gave the *Bluenose* crew time to make repairs to the gear that had broken during the first race. Old age had made many parts brittle and unreliable.

*Bluenose* looked more like her old self in the second race, which was sailed in moderate winds off Gloucester on October 13. Ignoring the superstition that sailors sometimes attach to the number 13, *Bluenose* won easily by more than 12 minutes.

After the second race, the Americans, believing that *Bluenose* had won because she carried more ballast than the rules allowed, demanded that her waterline be checked.

W. J. Roué, her designer, was on hand to see that the measurement was properly taken. True enough, *Bluenose's* waterline was 34.8 metres (114 feet), .6 of a metre (two feet) longer than permissible. While it probably had made no difference at all in the outcome of the race, the Americans insisted that an adjustment be made before the next race. So ballast was removed from *Bluenose* to bring the length of her waterline to 34.2 metres (112 feet).

Unfortunately for the Americans, the change seemed to make *Bluenose* sail better than ever. She won the third race at

*Bluenose* leading *Thebaud* in the 1938 series.

Gloucester by more than 6 minutes.

The schooners sailed down to Boston for the fourth race, with *Bluenose* ahead in the series two races to one. The race began on October 24 in winds gusting from 8 to 25 knots. Early in the race *Bluenose* got a 12-metre (40-foot-long) tear in her staysail. Fortunately she had a sailmaker aboard who was able to make the repairs quickly.

With 5 kilometres (3 miles) to go, *Bluenose* was in the lead when she was struck by a more serious misfortune. Her fore-topmast stay snapped, making it impossible to control the top-sail, which flopped about in the wind. By the time the damage could be repaired, *Thebaud* had caught up, going on to win by 5 minutes. Now the series was tied at two races each.

Even though she lost the fourth race, *Bluenose* set a record during the first leg of the course. She reached a speed of 14.5

knots, a record speed on a fixed course for a vessel powered only by sails.

The fifth and deciding race was set for October 26 off Gloucester on what was known as the Cape Ann triangle. The excitement and suspense were intense. For the two crews the tension must have been almost unbearable.

If *Thebaud* won it would mean that the Americans would hold all the great international racing trophies, the America's Cup, the Lipton Trophy, and the International Fishermen's Trophy. It was do or die for *Bluenose*. This was the final race. There would be no tomorrows.

The race began under overcast skies in winds of 15-18 knots out of the west. *Bluenose* took the lead in the first leg with *Thebaud* close on her tail. It stayed that way through to the final dash for home.

Under full sail, racing down the wind in the final stretch for the finish line, *Bluenose* held on to a small lead. *Thebaud* was barely three minutes behind her, and quite capable of catching up quickly should *Bluenose* make a slip.

Then *Bluenose*, making her last tack across the wind before crossing the finish line, had her topsail halyard break, making control of the topsail extremely difficult. But it was too late for *Thebaud* to take advantage. *Bluenose's* lead was enough, and she crossed the finish line 2 minutes and 50 seconds in the lead.

She had won, and all the questions about her age and sailing ability had now been answered. She was still the best, her mastery of sea and wind proven once and for all. Proudly she sailed back to Lunenburg, still Queen of the North Atlantic.

This 1938 series was the last of the races between the great fishing schooners of the North Atlantic. For a while, even the memories of their great achievements faded away, as the world plunged into the terrible darkness of World War II.

# CHAPTER 13

## DEATH OF A QUEEN

The 1938 series marked more than the end of international schooner racing on the North Atlantic. It marked the beginning of the end for *Bluenose* herself.

Diesel engines had been installed in 1936, making it possible for *Bluenose* to fish year-round and sell in both the salt cod and fresh fish markets. But so unprofitable had the fishing trade become by the late 1930s, that even working full time she could not earn enough to pay off her debts.

Captain Angus Walters had retired from the sea in 1939, but he remained a part owner of the schooner. His attachment to *Bluenose* was intense, and he could not bear to see her sold. Somehow he managed to raise $7,000 to keep her from the auction block, and hoped that a combination of fishing and coastal trade would earn enough to keep her in Lunenburg.

The outbreak of war in 1939 ended any such hope. German warships and submarines prowling the Atlantic made it unsafe to fish on the Banks. Even coastal trade was risky. *Bluenose* remained tied to her dock in Lunenburg.

Finally there was no choice but to sell her. Angus Walters had hoped enough money could be raised to keep *Bluenose* as a memorial to the skills of Nova Scotia shipbuilders and seamen. Little interest was shown in such a venture because

**Heeled over with her lee rail under, *Bluenose* dashes for victory.**

Canadians now were totally caught up in the war. Circumstances demanded far greater sacrifices than the loss of a sailing vessel. Schooners could wait; survival could not.

And so, in 1942 *Bluenose* was sold to a firm called the West Indies Trading Company. She was stripped of her masts and rigging, and went to the Caribbean where she was used to carry such products as rum and sugar from island to island.

There are stories that she sometimes carried other cargoes, such as explosives and ammunition, in runs between Cuba and Florida. It was wartime, and no doubt such runs proved to be profitable for her, even if dangerous.

On one of these runs she is said to have been stopped at sea by a German submarine. According to the story, the captain of the U-Boat spoke to the crew of the schooner in perfect English:

"You are *Bluenose* out of Havana bound for Port Everglades," he said. "If I didn't love that boat, I'd shell you right now."

The schooner was allowed to proceed unharmed.

Stories such as these, and there are many that have been told over the years, unfortunately have not been confirmed.

Still, they are interesting and add to the colourful *Bluenose* legend.

Finally the old schooner ran out of luck. In January, 1946, she struck a coral reef near the island of Haiti in the West Indies. The crew got off safely, but *Bluenose*, her tired hull unable to withstand yet another beating, broke apart and sank in the warm Caribbean waters. Nothing remained of her.

It is a curious fact that all of the great schooners that raced for the International Fishermen's Trophy met tragic ends similar to that of *Bluenose*. *Columbia* was lost with all hands in a gale off Sable Island in 1927. *Henry Ford* went down in 1928 on Whale's Back Reef near the Newfoundland coast. In 1935, *Elsie* sank in the Gulf of St. Lawrence, and in 1948, two years after *Bluenose* went down, *Thebaud* was tom to pieces on the coast of Venezuela. A watery grave had claimed them all.

In Nova Scotia, news of the loss of *Bluenose* came as a shock. Some called it a national tragedy, and said that Canadians should be ashamed for having allowed *Bluenose* to be sold in the first place. All this interest came too late to be of any help. Only memories of the great schooner remained now.

For a year or so there was talk of building another *Bluenose* from the plans of the first, but few besides Angus Walters were really serious about such a project, and fewer still were willing to put up the money. Fifteen years passed without any action, and it seemed unlikely that the idea of another *Bluenose* would take hold again.

Then, in 1960, the Smith and Rhuland shipyards in Lunenburg got a contract to build an exact replica of the famous 18th century British square rigger, the *Bounty*, for a Hollywood film, *Mutiny on the Bounty*. So great was the interest in this project, and so fine a job did the Lunenburg shipwrights do, that Nova Scotians were convinced another *Bluenose* should be built. The problem of money to pay for the project was resolved when the Oland Company of Halifax offered to sponsor the new schooner.

The new *Bluenose* was not to be a fishing vessel, of course, nor would it be expected to race. Those days were gone. But it would be a fine memorial to the great salt bankers of the past, as well as an excellent tourist attraction. Fees from tours and charters would offset the costs of maintenance and operation.

On July 24, 1963, Angus Walters' dream finally came true when *Bluenose II* was launched from the slips at the Smith and Rhuland yards in Lunenburg. The wiry south shore skipper, now in his 70s, was present for the occasion, as was W. J. Roué, her world famous designer. *Bluenose II* cost $300,000 to build, compared to $35,000 to build the original back in 1921.

The building of *Bluenose II* ensured that the legend of the great schooner would not die. Since 1963, hundreds of thousands of visitors from around the world have walked her decks and been told of the feats of her famous ancestor.

Today, with Lunenburg still her home port, *Bluenose II* operates as a tourist attraction for the province of Nova Scotia, running excursions and charters from her summer berth at Privateer's Wharf in Halifax. She flies the Canadian flag, and has represented Canada and Nova Scotia at World Fairs in Montreal in 1967 and Vancouver in 1986. She has visited almost every port on the eastern coasts of Canada and the United States, and has taken part in several international

*Bluenose II*

parades of tall ships. She has made the name *Bluenose* known in every corner of the world.

*Bluenose II* carries slightly more sail than *Bluenose*, but otherwise their dimensions are essentially the same. Her hull is made of oak, and her masts of Douglas fir. Deck hatches are made of mahogany. She has a crew of 18, made up of five officers, a Chief Steward, and 12 seamen. Below decks she has modern twin engines which give her speeds up to 10 knots. Under full sail in a good breeze, she has logged 18 knots.

While *Bluenose II* does not work the Grand Banks or race, those who have sailed with her on several long voyages, including the trip through the Panama Canal to the Pacific and up to San Francisco and Vancouver, say she is just as seaworthy and capable as her namesake in all kinds of weather.

Indeed, there are some old sailors who believe that if *Bluenose II* were to race, and if there were to be another challenger, she would still prove to be the best, another Queen of the North Atlantic.

# EPILOGUE

Under a mackerel sky a fishing schooner ghosts along in light winds, her fore and main booms swung wide, or "wrung out" as sailors would say, in order that her sails may catch every bit of breeze.

Her skipper, pacing the after deck, feels the first breath of a rising wind. He senses a cold nor'easter in the making.

"Up foresail! Set topsails and jib!" he commands, and the crew is quick to respond. Shifting currents and sudden squalls leave no room for hesitation when the "Old Man" decides the course of action.

"Get her on the starboard tack!" he orders.

With the schooner's holds nearly full of cod, split and salted down, with a storm rising and heavy seas to come, the skipper decides it is time to make a run for home.

"Hard-a-starboard," he shouts to the helmsman, and the big schooner sets her course to the southwest, on the long reach down to Lunenburg and safe harbour.

That's what it was like to be on the Grand Banks in those days long past, when the great salt bank schooners sped gracefully between wind and sea in the quest for fish in the cold North Atlantic.

And the greatest sail carrier of them all was *Bluenose*, the undisputed Queen of the great schooners that plied the oceans in the heyday of the saltwater fishing ships.

Whether she was running down the wind homeward bound, with a spray of salt water touching her lee rail, or close hauled and biting into the teeth of a strong sou'wester, *Bluenose* caught the imagination of sailors and landlubbers alike, and to this day her image stirs the hearts of all who are drawn irresistibly to the sea and ships.

# INTERNATIONAL FISHERMEN'S TROPHY RACES: 1921 - 1938

| Year | SHIP | CAPTAIN | RACE 1 | RACE 2 | RACE 3 | RACE 4 | RACE 5 |
|------|------|---------|--------|--------|--------|--------|--------|
| 1921 | *Bluenose* | A. Walters | 1st | 1st | | | |
|      | *Elsie* | M. Welch | 2nd | 2nd | | | |
| 1922 | *Bluenose* | A. Walters | Declared | 2nd | 1st | 1st | |
|      | *Henry Ford* | C. Morrissey | No Race | 1st | 2nd | 2nd | |
| 1923 | *Bluenose* | A. Walters | 1st | 1st* | Race awarded to *Columbia*. | | |
|      | *Columbia* | B. Pine | 2nd | 2nd | Series ruled "No Contest" | | |
| 1931 | *Bluenose* | A. Walters | 1st | 1st | | | |
|      | *Thebaud* | B. Pine | 2nd | 2nd | | | |
| 1938 | *Bluenose* | A. Walters | 2nd | 1st | 1st | 2nd | 1st |
|      | *Thebaud* | B. Pine | 1st | 2nd | 2nd | 1st | 2nd |

## OTHER CHALLENGE RACES

| Year | SHIP | CAPTAIN | RACE 1 | RACE 2 | RACE 3 | RACE 4 | RACE 5 |
|------|------|---------|--------|--------|--------|--------|--------|
| 1926 | *Bluenose* | A. Walters | 1st | 1st | | | |
|      | *Thebaud* | M. Crouse | 2nd | 2nd | | | |
| 1930 | *Bluenose* | A. Walters | 2nd | 2nd | | | |
|      | *Thebaud* | B. Pine | 1st | 1st | | | |
|      | (Lipton Cup) | | | | | | |

# GLOSSARY OF SAILING TERMS

| | |
|---|---|
| AFT | toward the stern of a vessel. |
| ALEE | away from the direction of the wind (also see lee). |
| ASTERN | behind a vessel. |
| BALLAST | additional weight placed in the hull of a vessel to improve its stability. |
| BEAM | the width of a ship at its widest point. |
| BEFORE THE WIND | in the same direction as the wind is going. |
| BELOW | beneath the deck. |
| BOOM | a long spar extending from a mast which holds the foot or bottom of a sail. |
| BOW | the forward part of a vessel. |
| BOWSPRIT | a spar which extends out from the bow of a vessel. |
| BUOY | a float anchored in the water to mark a channel or indicate danger. |
| COME ABOUT | turn the bow of a boat through the eye of the wind, i.e. the direction from which the wind is blowing. (Also see tack). |
| CLOSE-HAULED | sailing as close as possible into the wind. |
| DORY | small, narrow flat-bottomed boat used in the sea fisheries. |
| DRAUGHT (DRAFT) | the depth of a vessel's keel below the waterline. |
| EYE OF THE WIND | the direction from which the wind is blowing. |
| FATHOM | a marine measure of depth equal to 1.8 metres or 6 feet. |
| FORWARD | toward the bow. |
| GAFF | a spar used to support the top edge of a fore-and-aft sail. |
| GHOSTING | sailing with little or no wind. |
| HALYARD | a rope used to raise and lower sails. |
| HELM | the steering wheel or tiller of a vessel. |
| HULL | the main body of a vessel. |
| JIB | a triangular sail set forward of the foremast. |
| JUMBO | a triangular sail set forward of the foremast, but inside the jib. |

| | |
|---|---|
| KEEL | the lowest part of a vessel beneath the hull. |
| KNOT | a nautical measure of speed equal to about 1.15 miles per hour or 2 kilometers per hour. |
| LEE | the side away from the direction in which the wind is blowing. (Also see alee). |
| LEEWARD | the direction away from that in which the wind is blowing. (Also see lee and alee). |
| MAST | tall vertical spar that supports the sails, booms, gaffs and lines of a sailing vessel. |
| MAINSAIL | the sail set on the mainmast. |
| OFF THE WIND | sailing with the wind coming from astern. (Also see running). |
| PORT | the left side of a vessel looking toward the bow. The direction to the left. |
| RUNNING | sailing with the wind astern. (Also see off the wind). |
| RIGGING | the system of ropes, tackle and gear used to support and control the masts and sails. |
| SHEETS | lines used to adjust a sail. |
| SHROUDS | fixed ropes or lines that support a mast at the side. |
| SPARS | a general name given to the masts, booms and gaffs that support the sails. |
| STARBOARD | the right side of a vessel looking towards the bow. The direction to the right. |
| STAYS | fixed ropes or lines that support the masts from forward to aft, i.e. front to rear. |
| STAYSAILS | triangular or four-sided sails set in addition to and inside a vessel's other sails; e.g. the fisherman's staysail - set forward of the mainsail. |
| STERN | the rear of a vessel. |
| TACK | the way a vessel is sailing with respect to the wind. A boat is said to be on the starboard tack if the wind is coming from the right. |
| TOPSAIL | a sail set above the gaff. |
| WATERLINE | the line on the hull of a vessel to which the water rises. |
| WINDWARD | the direction from which the wind is blowing. |

# PHOTO CREDITS

Reprinted by Permission of the National Art Limited Halifax, N.S. p. 8, 9, 11,14,15, 19, 21, 30, 33, 34, 38, 39, 42, 44, 47, 52, 67, 70 Jeanne Frances Robinson p. 24 Samuel F Manning, Azor Vinenneau (Shipbuilding Tools) p. 30-31 Samuel F. Manning p. 28-29 Maritime Museum of the Atlantic Halifax, N.S. p. 10, 30 City of Toronto Archives, Globe and Mail Collection #30025 p. 60 Allen Ward p. 73

# NOTES

Chapter 1 p. 8. Reprinted by permission of the Public Archives of Nova Scotia, MG 9, No. 95, p. 8. *How Bluenose Was Designed* by W.J. Roué, from the *Halifax Herald*, Dec. 30, 1923.

Chapter 4 p. 24, 26, 27. Courtesy of *The Chronicle-Herald Halifax*, *The Bluenose Story*, July 23, 1963. Reprinted by permission of the Public Archives of Nova Scotia, MG 9, No. 95, p. 11 *How Bluenose Was Designed* by W.J. Roué, from the Halifax Herald, Dec. 30, 1923. MG 100, Vol. 216, No. 1 a-b. Letter from E.A. Bell to A. Merkle, Nov. 19, 1947.

Chapter 11 p. 65. Brian Backman, *Bluenose*, Toronto: McClelland and Stewart Ltd., 1965, p. 19.

Chapter 13 p. 71. Courtesy of *The Chronicle-Herald Halifax*. From a review of *War Years of Canada's Bluenose*, May 24, 1975.

# INDEX